Daydreams Make Dreams Kindergarten, 2001

I was 5 years old at the time, and boy did I have a huge imagination! That's normal for anyone my age right? Daydreaming was constant for me especially during assignments.

My Drawing Addiction First Grade, 2002

My brain was an ongoing reel of different kinds of stories, ideas and characters from the video games I grew up with. This lead me to create a mini comic series which I shared with my sister and friends. Their encouragement was enough for me to keep going. I was hooked on creating art. It was good for keeping me busy, but that has it's own consequences.

Oh no! my grades! First Grade, 2002

As you may have already guessed, my grades did suffer from it. I tried paying attention, but I never felt like it was interesting enough to retain the information. I found school such a chore to sit through which caused me to draw even more.

Focus... Just Focus First Grade, 2002

My mom was disappointed with my grades. She knew I could do better. My brother and sister made good grades, so why couldn't I? I tried hard but, I didn't feel engaged. I couldn't get the grades I wanted. I'd hear, "You just need to focus more," constantly. Things that came natural for other kids my age was a struggle for me.

Come Out Of Minzyland
First Grade, 2002

Throughout elementary, so many conferences happened between teachers and my parents. I had to put a stop to my obsessive sketching. Every conference was the same. "She seems to be in LA LA Land" one teacher would say. "She doesn't seem to care and is really disorganized" another would add. The pressure to focus more increased.

The Dark Years
Grade 6, 2008

My transition to middle school was definitely one of the hardest 3 years of my life. Although very tough, I feel my struggles helped my growth as a person.

Minzy The Artist
Grade 6, 2008

I was definitely that girl without a clique in middle school. I was either by myself or I was with the outcasts. No matter where I was, I was drawing. I created original characters and exotic worlds. Fun fact: I had a series that was 30 plus books long!

Bullying Isn't Okay!
Grade 8, 2010

At first I drew from boredom, but now it's different. I was now drawing because I was trying to escape the bullying. I struggled in class and this caused me to never ask questions when I didn't understand. My grades did drop and I eventually had to switch classes.

Lost Time
Grade 8, 2010

I'll never forget the days I had to stay after school for tutoring. It was torture! I felt trapped with in the walls of the classroom. It was a constant reminder that my struggles landed me here. I lost confidence in myself. I attended summer school and missed out on vacations and time with friends. Yeah it sucked...

Eliminate Distractions
Grade 9, 2011

During my first year of high school, I was forced to sit in the front row of every class. I was pulled out of class and placed in a different setting, for testing sessions. I never understood why. Apparently, it was to keep me from being distracted and help me focus better. (I personally never saw much of a difference).

Lost In Space
Grade 9, 2011

Strange events continued to happen. I was given random I.Q tests and I continued having personal meetings with my teachers about my grades. More parent teacher conferences too. I began feeling like a strange experiment. Why was I being treated like this, and not the other kids? I had more questions than answers.

Caution: Roadwork Ahead College Year, 2014

I have some bittersweet news! During my first year of college, I did put away my obssesive drawing habits and gave it my all. My grades did improve from my traditional D's to at least C's and B's. (For me that was an improvement at the time). My confidence came from my family and friends who believed I could do it.

A Mystery Is A foot
College Year, 2019

It was my sophomore year in college and I still wasn't getting the grades I wanted. I failed some classes and passed others. The conversations with my instructors had a similar pattern, "You seem very disconnected during lecture." I've heard this at least 100 times from teachers. I questioned what was really going on? Why did I keep hearing this?

Self Discovery
College Year, 2019

I did some research (and by some, I mean a lot)! I was told "Never let anyone label me," but there were some things I have noticed about myself that I wasn't afraid to admit. The truth was, I did have trouble focusing in certain situations and I did process information differently. I knew I needed answers and I needed them now.

ADHD!!! That`s It! College Year, 2020

After failing my internship (because of the same reasons I mentioned before), I was recommended a counselor. To be honest I didn't want to go but I was tired of hearing "Just focus and you will be okay", so I got evaluated and it turned out I was dealing with inattentive ADHD! I felt a mix of anxiety and relief! That day ADHD became part of my identity!

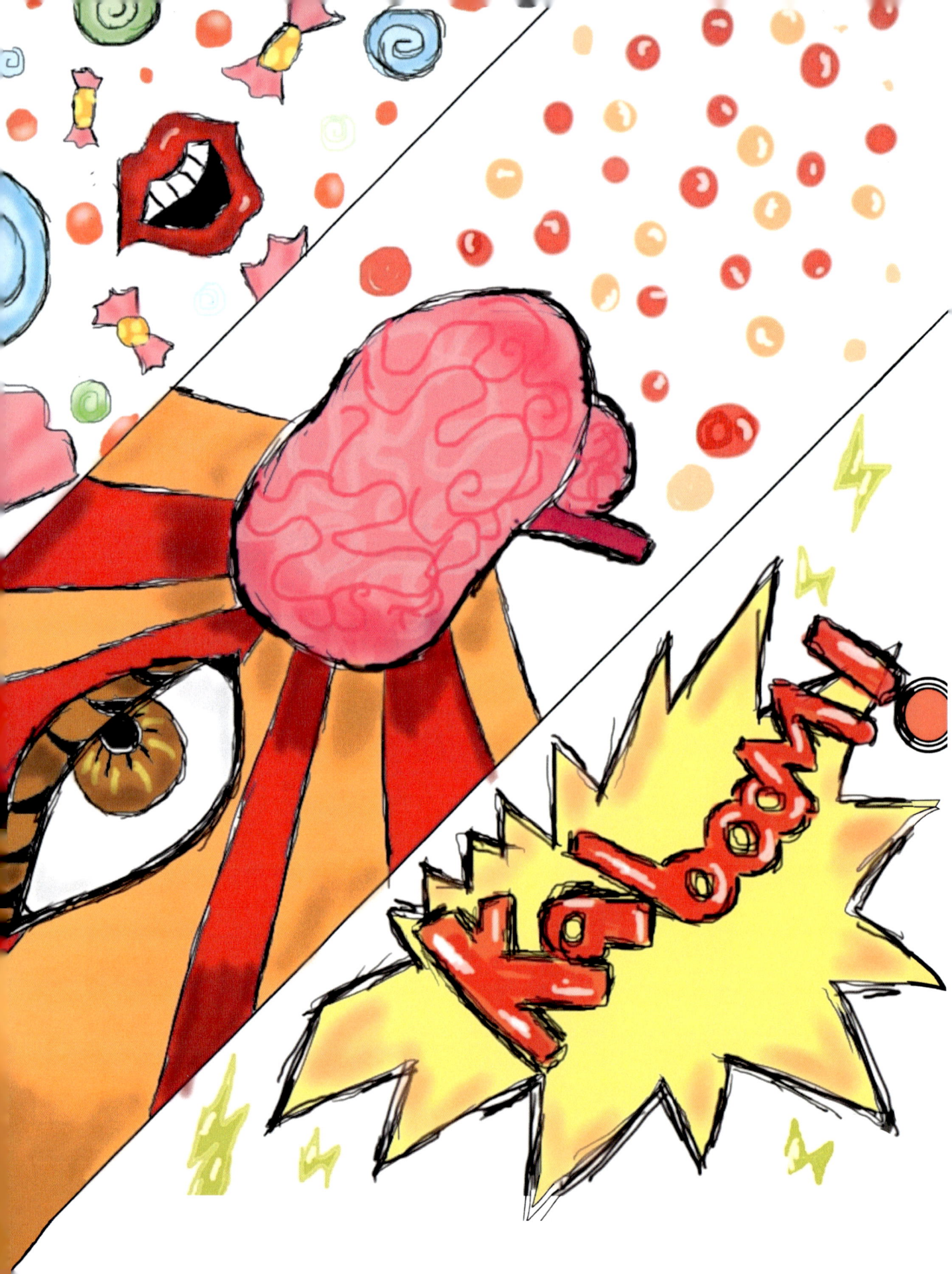

what is ADHD you ask?
College Year, 2021

My own summary of ADHD (Attention deficit hyper activity disorder) is that there are two main subtypes: Hyperactive is where a person is hyperactive. They may appear restless and have trouble sitting still. The inattentive subtype, (what I have) is where a person has trouble processing information and focusing. People with this type usually don't have the hyper active portion.

Tell yourself, I am smart!

Even though I have ADHD, that doesn't mean I cant comprehend anything. I can do that pretty well actually. I just have to learn different ways to make learning easier for me.

The Journey So Far!

The journey hasn't been easy. Discovering what I have is just the beginning. I may continue to have set backs and sometimes my progress will be delayed, but here is one thing. I will NEVER give up on me. I have come so far and as long as I am breathing, I know each day is another chance to get back up and try again because...

Copyright © 2021

Antz Productions Inc.

Author:
Jasmine "Minzy" Harris

Illustrator:
Jasmine "Minzy" Harris

All rights reserved. This book or any portion thereof may not be reproduced or used in any manner whatsoever without the express written permission of the publisher except for the use of brief quotations in a book review.

Printed in the United States of America.

Made in the USA
Columbia, SC
01 January 2022